GW00391830

For a Special Friend

A Heartwarmers™ Gift Book

WPL

For a Special Friend

A Heartwarmers™ Gift Book

©WPL 2002

Text by A. Fisher

Additional material by Howard Baker & Anne Dodds

Illustration by Dolen Corbridge - Advocate

Printed in China

Published by WPL 2002

ISBN 1-904264-02-6

For information on other Heartwarmers™ gift books, gifts and greetings cards, please contact

WPL

14 Victoria Ind. Est. Wales Farm Road
London W3 6UU UK

Tel: +44 (0) 208 993 7268 Fax: +44 (0) 208 993 8041
email: info@wpl.eu.com www.wpl.eu.com

This little book is just for you
as I wanted to say,
all the things that go unsaid
as life goes on each day.

I feel so lucky
you're my friend
and I really hope you know,
you'll always mean
the world to me
wherever I may go.

You always somehow
make me smile
and cheer me up
when I'm blue.
Life would not be
half as nice
if I did not
have you.

You smile away
my troubles,
you soothe away regret.
You're honest, kind
and cheerful
and I'm so glad we met.

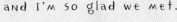

I always know
when things go right
my happiness you'll share,
and I know too
there are few like you,
true friends are very rare.

It's wonderful
to have a friend
who makes the effort to see
things from my own
point of view
and who looks out for me.

I know you'll always be there
at any time of day,
to listen and to understand
in your own special way.

You're there for me
to lean on
when things are getting tough,
and you've a shoulder
I can cry on
when I feel I've had enough.

When facing disappointment
heartbreak or pain,
I've always been able
to turn to you
again and again.

You can see when
I'm in trouble
even when I can't,
and you give me
really good advice
like the best Agony Aunt.

You've always
helped me see things
from a different point of view,
and your advice and guidance
is straightforward and true.

You've raised my spirits often
when I have felt depressed,
supported and encouraged me
when life has got me stressed.

Thanks for being so patient,
honest, loyal and kind.
You've been there
when I've needed you
and never seemed to mind.

Whatever I am facing,
whatever mountains
I have to scale,
knowing you believe in me
makes me feel I cannot fail.

I want to repay you for
all the kindness you have shown,
as you're one of
the nicest people
I have ever known.

You're such a
special person
with qualities so rare,
compassion,
understanding
and a warmth
beyond compare.

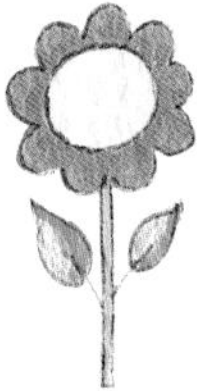

so when you need an ally,
who's reliable and true,
I hope that you will call on me
so I can be there for you.

If ever you're in trouble
or in need of a friend,
if you need a
shoulder to cry on,
on me you can depend.

I'll be there to share your joy
when things are going well,
but I'll never turn my back
when you're having a bad spell.

I'll be there to remind you
of the good things you deserve.
I'll be there to support you
if you ever lose your nerve.

I'll always be happy
to lend a helping hand,
and I hope you know
where you're concerned
I'll always understand.

I hope whatever happens
rainy days or sunshine,
wherever we go
and whatever we do
you'll be a special
friend of mine.

I am really grateful
for the friendship that we share.
You encourage me to try things
which, alone, I might not dare.

You've made my life
much happier
than it's ever been before,
and as I get to
know you better
I can't help
but like you more.

You're thoughtful
and considerate,
funny, wise and kind.
You've always been able
to make me laugh
and help me to unwind.

We know each other
so very well
and don't have to pretend
to put on airs and graces
or to follow any trend.

I know that you
and I as friends
can overcome any snags,
we'll always have each other
whether life brings us
riches or rags.

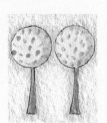

I look forward to the future
knowing you'll be there,
someone to guide me on my way
with love, support and care.

I believe I'm a better person
just for having known you.
You have qualities
I've learnt from –
you're down to earth
and true.

You have so
many talents,
you're practical
and smart,
but best of all
I think is that
you have the
biggest heart.

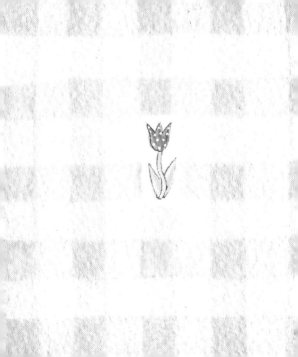

You're full of optimism,
generosity and grace,
and if everyone
had a friend like you
the world would be
a happier place.

The future is something
that we've yet to explore,
but with the two of us I'm sure
there'll be some fun in store.

I count myself as lucky
for I could travel far,
and never find
myself a friend
who's as special
as you are.

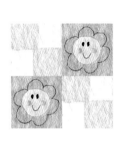

And I just wanted you to know
that there is no contest -
when it comes to
special friends
you really are the best!

A Heartwarmers™
Gift Book
WPL